The Apple Tree

The Apple Tree

A New Musical

MUSIC by *JERRY BOCK*

and

LYRICS by *SHELDON HARNICK*

Based on stories by

MARK TWAIN, FRANK R. STOCKTON and JULES FEIFFER

Book by SHELDON HARNICK and JERRY BOCK

Additional book material by JEROME COOPERSMITH

Random House NEW YORK

Photographs by courtesy of Freidman-Abeles

MANUFACTURED IN THE UNITED STATES OF AMERICA

THE APPLE TREE *was first presented on October 18, 1966, by Stuart Ostrow at the Sam S. Shubert Theatre in New York City, with the following cast:*

(In order of appearance)

THE DIARY OF ADAM AND EVE

Adam	Alan Alda
Eve	Barbara Harris
Snake	Larry Blyden

THE LADY OR THE TIGER?

Balladeer	Larry Blyden
King Arik	Marc Jordan
Princess Barbara	Barbara Harris
Prisoner	Jay Norman
Prisoner's Bride	Jaclynn Villamil
Guard	Robert Klein
Nadjira	Carmen Alvarez
Captain Sanjar	Alan Alda
King Arik's Court	Jackie Cronin, Barbara Lang, Mary Louise, Michael Davis, Neil F. Jones

PASSIONELLA

Narrator	Larry Blyden
Ella and Passionella	Barbara Harris
Mr. Fallible	Robert Klein
Producer	Marc Jordan
Flip, The Prince, Charming	Alan Alda

Subway Riders, El Morocco Patrons, Flip's Fans

FOLLOWING, MOVIE SET CREW	Carmen Alvarez, Jackie Cronin, Michael Davis, Neil F. Jones, Marc Jordan, Robert Klein, Barbara Lang, Mary Louise, Jay Norman, Jaclynn Villamil

Additional Musical Staging by Herbert Ross
Choreography by Lee Theodore
Production and Costume Design by Tony Walton
Lighting by Jean Rosenthal
Musical Direction and Vocal Arrangements by Elliot Lawrence
Orchestrations by Eddie Sauter
Entire Production Directed by Mike Nichols

Synopsis of Scenes

The Diary of Adam and Eve

Time: Saturday, June first
Place: Eden

The Lady or the Tiger?

Time: A long time ago
Place: A semi-barbaric kingdom

Passionella

Time: Now
Place: Here

Musical Numbers

Part I

The Diary of Adam and Eve

Song	Performer
"Here in Eden"	EVE
"Feelings"	EVE
"Eve"	ADAM
"Friends"	EVE
"The Apple Tree" ("Forbidden Fruit")	SNAKE
"Beautiful, Beautiful World"	ADAM
"It's a Fish"	ADAM
"Go to Sleep Whatever You Are"	EVE
"What Makes Me Love Him"	EVE

Part II

The Lady or the Tiger?

Song	Performer
"I'll Tell You a Truth"	BALLADEER
"Make Way"	KING ARIK and COURT
"Forbidden Love"	PRINCESS BARBARA and SANJAR
"In Gaul"	PRINCESS BARBARA and SANJAR
"Forbidden Fruit"	BALLADEER
"I've Got What You Want"	PRINCESS BARBARA
"Tiger, Tiger"	PRINCESS BARBARA
"Make Way" (*reprise*)	KING'S COURT
"Which Door?"	COMPANY
"I'll Tell You a Truth" (*reprise*)	BALLADEER

Part III

PASSIONELLA

"Oh, to Be a Movie Star"	ELLA
"Gorgeous"	PASSIONELLA
"(Who, Who, Who, Who) Who Is She?"	COMPANY
"I Know"	PASSIONELLA
"Wealth"	PASSIONELLA
"You Are Not Real"	FLIP and COMPANY
"George L."	ELLA and GEORGE

PART I

The Diary of Adam and Eve

Based on *The Diary of Adam and Eve*
by Mark Twain

As the curtain rises, the lights come up gradually to reveal ADAM *asleep on the ground. The garden is symbolized quite sparingly with a tree, a mound of flowers, and a scrim behind which we can faintly see an apple tree in the distance.*

A voice is heard as the music slowly fades.

VOICE Adam—Adam, wake up. You are the first man. It shall be your task to name all the creatures in the Garden of Eden. You may eat the fruit of the trees and the fields, but stay away from the apple tree on the other side of the hill. Adam, wake up.

ADAM (*Stirring slowly*) Just give me five more minutes.

VOICE (*Booming now*) Adam! Wake up!

ADAM (*He wakes up and rises to his haunches*) —name the creatures— (*Yawning and mumbling*) —well, I might as well get it over with. (*Rises*) I, Adam, by virtue of the authority vested in me, do hereby name all you creatures flying around in the sky—flyers. (*A musical chord sounds*) And you things crawling on the ground I name—crawlers. (*Chord*) And you things swimming around down there are swimmers, and you're growlers, and you're hoppers. Oh, my, there are thousands. I better start taking notes or I'll get everything all mixed up. (*To the audience*) This is the first day, Adamtime. Note: (*Chord*) Today I named the flyers, crawlers, swimmers, growlers, and hoppers. Further note: There are creatures here of every conceivable kind, but I, Adam, am the sole and single man. (*He smiles with pride, savoring the word*) Single. That word has a fine, open ring to it. (*He grabs his rib and winces in pain*) Ahh. Now what? (*A mound rolls onstage with* EVE *asleep on it.* ADAM *turns and goes to it. He circles it in curiosity*) I'll name it later.

(ADAM *exits and the music swells. The lights slowly change and* EVE *wakes, instinctively reaching out for a companion. She sits up and is struck with bewilderment and wonder*)

EVE (*Staring out front and sitting up*) Sunlight? Hummingbirds? Lions? Where am I? I? What am I? (*The music fades as she looks down and is startled by the sight of herself*) Oh!! (*She studies herself carefully, running her fingers over her face and hair*) Whatever I am, I'm certainly a beautiful one. (*She laughs suddenly*) It's very peculiar—but I feel like—an experiment. (*Laughing again*) In fact, it would be impossible to feel more like an experiment than I do. Then am I the whole experiment? (*She carefully surveys herself again*) I don't think so. I better start making notes right now. Some instinct tells me these details are going to be important to the historian some day. (*She gets up on her haunches and moves off the mound*) Saturday, June first. Note: (*The music to "Here in Eden" begins*) I arrived, feeling exactly like an experiment. Around me there is an incredible profusion of the most delightful objects. (*Singing*)

So many creatures,
So many things,

Each wondrous object is beautiful and striking,
And I see nothing that isn't to my liking
Here in Eden.

There's plums and peaches
And pears and grapes
So ripe and juicy and utterly inviting.
I find the apples especially exciting
Here in Eden.

As for me,
I can see
I was meant to rejoice
In the round,
Vibrant sound
Of my own voice.

It's all so perfect
And so ideal,
And yet I do have one tiny reservation:
There's nothing handy for making conversation
Here in Eden.

How'd I come?
Where'm I from?
What's my ultimate aim?
I don't know.
Even so,
I'm glad I came.

It's all so lovely
I may just weep.
I love this garden and ev'rything that's in it,
And something tells me to treasure ev'ry minute,

Blossom and bud,
Mountain and mud,
I know I'll be happy,
Perfectly happy,
Here in Eden.

(She hugs herself in delight and gazes about as ADAM *enters with a fish, which he is mumbling at. They both stop and stare at each other)*

EVE Drop that pickerel, you monster! *(He dives for his tree)* Put it back. *(She reaches down for a rock lying about.* ADAM *is up the tree by now)* Did you hear me?

ADAM *(From the tree)* What do you think you're doing?

EVE *(Startled by his voice)* You can talk!

ADAM Get away from here!

EVE *(Her compassion for the pickerel makes her brave and she crosses to the tree)* Throw that pickerel back!

ADAM What pickerel?

EVE That pickerel in your hand.

ADAM That's a swimmer.

EVE A pickerel!

ADAM Swimmer!

EVE Pickerel.

ADAM Swimmer.

EVE (*She holds up the rock in her hand*) What's this?

ADAM A clod.

EVE Well, if you don't throw that pickerel back, I'm going to clod you right out of that tree.

(*She throws the rock and picks up some more to throw*)

ADAM Wait!

(*He throws the fish over her head. She puts the rocks down, crosses, and picks up the fish*)

EVE (*Hugging the fish soothingly*) And don't you ever do that again, you bully. (*She crosses to the mound, picks up the rope tail, and pulls the mound offstage.* ADAM *leaps off the tree and picks up three rocks. He is about to throw them after her when she instantly appears*) I'm warning you!

(*He pretends to juggle the rocks as she exits again. He puts the rocks on the tree mound and starts talking to the audience*)

ADAM Second day, Adamtime. Note: I'm worried. Yesterday that new long-haired creature kept hanging around and following me. However, I believe I've hidden myself so cleverly, it probably thinks I've left the garden.

(*He climbs the tree, gets a towel off a branch, and covers himself.* EVE *enters with a brisk, businesslike walk*)

EVE (*Suddenly turning to him*) I must talk to you!

ADAM (*Throwing down the towel*) About what?

EVE (*At a loss*) Oh, I just like to talk. Don't you like to talk?

ADAM Not particularly. (*Hitting at her with the towel*) Go away. Go away.

EVE (*Standing her ground*) Please come down. There *is* something, and I think it's immensely important.

ADAM What?

EVE Will you come down?

ADAM (*Thinks for a moment*) All right. I think I'm stronger than you.

EVE Oh, I'm sure you are.

ADAM (*Jumping out of the tree*) Now, what did you want to talk about?

EVE (*Moving to him*) About us.

ADAM You stay over there! (*She moves back*) What's us?

EVE That's a name I thought of. It means you and me.

ADAM What's so important about us?

EVE I think we've both been put here for a great and noble experiment!

(She moves to him again)

ADAM I told you to stay over there!

EVE Sorry.

(She moves back)

ADAM Go on.

EVE *(Turning to him)* What?

ADAM I said go on!

EVE *(Edging over to him)* As I was saying—I think I'm the main part of this experiment, but you have a share in it, too.

ADAM Oh, that's very generous of you. What makes you think you and I have anything in common?

EVE *(Moving all the way to him)* Well, for one thing, you're the only other animal that can talk!

ADAM *(Backing away)* That's how much you know! So can—so can— *(Looking around for the illustration)* so can that flyer up there.

(He is pointing out front)

EVE *(Looking out front)* Where?

ADAM In that tree.

EVE *(Staring hard)* You mean that parrot? I didn't know parrots could talk!

ADAM Well, they can. Why do you call it a parrot?

EVE Because it looks like a parrot.

ADAM Well, not to me it doesn't. It looks like a loud-mouthed fat-beak.

EVE *(Laughing condescendingly)* Nevertheless, it's a parrot.

ADAM What makes you so positive?

EVE I just happen to have this talent. The minute I set eyes on an animal, I know what it is. I don't have to think. The right name comes out by inspiration. So far, you're the only exception.

ADAM *(He thinks for a moment, then fires the following questions at her as fast as he can. She answers with equal, and casual, rapidity)* What's that?

EVE A horse.

ADAM That?

EVE Bull.

ADAM That?

EVE Goat.

ADAM That?

EVE Elk.

ADAM That?

EVE Wolf.

ADAM That?

EVE Duck.

ADAM (*Exasperated*) You're just guessing!

EVE I'm not guessing. Those are their names, because—

BOTH —that's what they look like.

EVE Yes.

ADAM How old are you?

EVE (*Figuring it out*) Two days.

ADAM You'll never make it to four.

EVE (*Moving to him*) Oh, dear, I've hurt your feelings.

ADAM Ridiculous.

EVE (*Moving to him at the tree*) Yes, I have. I can tell. I'm so sorry.

ADAM *(Turning his back to her)* Well, don't be, because you're wrong. Anyway, I can't waste any more time here. I have to go empty the four-pronged white-squirter.

EVE You mean the cow?

ADAM Thank you very much!
(He exits)

EVE Somehow we got off on the wrong foot. I seem to aggravate it. I think it's a reptile. But I do wonder what it's for. I never see it do anything. Nothing seems to interest it—except resting. It's a man! If it *is* a man, then, it isn't an *it,* is it? No. It should be: Nominative: He. Dative: Him. Possessive: His'n. *(The music to "Feelings" begins)* I think that's right. It gets harder and harder to concentrate ever since I met the reptile. Just thinking about him gives me the most distracting sensations. *(Singing)*

Feelings are tumbling over feelings,
Feelings I do not understand,
And I am more than slightly worried
That they are getting out of hand.

Sometimes they happen in my stomach,
Sometimes they happen on my skin.
What is the name of this condition
That I am in?

If I'm objective and observant,
If I can keep an even keel,
I'll be the first to pin a name to
What I'm the very first to feel.

(The lights reveal a glowing bed of coals. EVE, *coughing, kneels by them, fanning the flames)*

Tuesday, June fourth. Special note. I believe I've finally discovered something that will interest him. It happened while I was trying to bore a hole in one stick with another stick.

(As she gazes raptly at the fire, ADAM *enters. He stops, sniffs the air, and traces the curious odor to its source, the fire)*

ADAM What's that?

EVE *(Not at all snidely)* What does it look like to you?

ADAM Pink dust.

EVE Its name is fire.

ADAM How did it come?

EVE I made it.

ADAM What are those?

EVE Fire-coals.

*(*ADAM *reaches down to pick one up.* EVE *watches. He drops it quickly, glares at* EVE, *and hurries offstage, trying not to reveal the fact that his fingers are killing him)*

EVE *(Sadly) Nothing* interests him. *(The music to "Feelings" begins again.* EVE *sings)*

I am the first to face this problem.
I am the first to have this dream.

How can I harness his attention?
How can I harvest his esteem?
Am I sufficiently attractive?
Should I do something with my hair?
(*She holds a strand out*)
Is there some tidbit that will please him?
What should I wear?
What is the source of this congestion
That I must learn to rise above?
Is there a name for this condition?
Yes, there's a name. . . .
And it is hell!

(*Blackout. The lights restore on* ADAM, *who is carrying a plank to construct some primitive shelter. The tree is gone, and there are other planks onstage*)

ADAM Sixth day, Adamtime. (*He drops the plank*) The naming goes recklessly on. I get no chance to name anything myself. The new creature names everything that comes along before I can get in a protest. And always on the same pretext—says it looks like the thing. For instance, take the great waterfall—the finest thing in the garden, I think. The new creature calls it "Niagara Falls." Why? Says it *looks* like Niagara Falls. Now that's not a reason. That's pure waywardness and imbecility. (*He begins to cross, but stops and returns with an afterthought*) And another thing. I'm not used to anything coming so close up to me. It makes me feel hampered and, uh, somewhat—anxious. (*He is covering over his confusion with a casual air. He tests the wind direction with a wet finger*) Uh, cloudy today. Wind in the east. I think we'll have rain. (*He crosses and gets a wooden tub and bowl)* We? Where did I get that word? Oh. Well, I don't care about "we"—I'm going to build *me* a dry-top.

(He sets up the planks tripod style and is busily at work as EVE *enters in a gay and cheerful mood)*

EVE Good morning. What are you doing? *(He hears her through all this but continues work)* Can I help? Are you hungry?

(She has an apple that she tosses in the air. He ignores her until the crunch from the bite she takes makes him turn. He grabs her, forces her down, and pulls the apple away)

ADAM *(In a panic)* Give me that—spit it out—come on. Where'd you get that?

EVE *(Fighting back)* Help! Help! *(After he has taken the apple)* From that tree.

ADAM Are you sure it's not from over the hill?

EVE Positive. *(He whistles in relief, rises, and crosses to the tub)* I don't understand.

ADAM *(Pointing upstage)* Those apples are forbidden.

EVE Why?

ADAM Because they're dangerous. If we eat those apples—something terrible will happen.

EVE What?

ADAM I don't know.

EVE (*Rises*) Maybe we should just go find out.

ADAM (*Leaping to bar her way*) Stay away from that tree, numskull!

EVE (*Stiffly*) My name happens to be Eve.

ADAM (*Crossing to the hut*) I have no objections.

EVE (*Following him*) In the future, kindly use my name when you wish to speak to me, or when you wish to call me. That's what it's for.

ADAM Then it's superfluous.
(*Puts a peg into the planks*)

EVE (*Despite her pique*) Superfluous! What a beautiful word! And it's so large! I'm proud of you . . . really I am. (*To the audience*) Superfluous! I don't think I've ever used it. (*To him*) Where did it come from?

ADAM (*Who has been watching her*) I don't know. I just kind of made it up. I was standing here looking at you, and I said to myself, "It looks superfluous."
(*He picks up his bowl and his stone*)

EVE (*Moving in closer*) I'm not an "it." (*Not angrily; she enjoys explaining*) I'm a "she."

ADAM (*Turning to her*) Ah, well, I wish *she* would go

play with the other animals, and I wish *she* would stop talking so much, because *we* have work to do.

(He turns upstage)

EVE Can't I help?

ADAM *(Not even looking at her)* No. She'd only be superfluous.

(He sits in the hut and begins to carve the bowl. The lights change to a stormy blue and the "rain music" begins)

EVE *(Reacting and putting a hand out)* I think I felt a drop.

ADAM *(Sticking a hand out of the hut)* It's starting to rain.

EVE May I come in?

ADAM It's crowded.

EVE I don't mind.

ADAM I mind.

EVE Why do you hate me so much? I just can't understand it! I'm a very interesting person. And if you'd only talk to me nicely, I could be twice as interesting.

(She begins to cry. ADAM *looks at her with great curiosity and interest)*

ADAM What are you doing?

EVE Nothing.

ADAM Yes, you are. You're raining, too!

EVE I'm crying. But don't let it disturb you.
(She turns away from him)

ADAM It doesn't, but . . . well . . . I don't like to see it. So . . .

EVE *(Eagerly turning to him)* Yes?

ADAM So either stop it, or go rain somewhere else.
(Now EVE *truly wails, walks away, and sits on the ground)*

ADAM *(Puts the bowl down and goes to her. With great exasperation)* All right. All right. Come on in.

EVE I don't want to.

ADAM Why not?

EVE It'll be too crowded.

ADAM I'll make room.

EVE Are you sure?

ADAM I'm sure.
(She goes into the hut; he follows. When they are both seated in the hut she leans on his shoulder)

Barbara Harris as PRINCESS BARBARA, Carmen Alvarez as NADJIRA, and Alan Alda as CAPTAIN SANJAR.

EVE What's your name?

ADAM What do I look like? Wait. My name is Adam.

EVE Adam . . . Adam . . . that sound is pleasanter in my ears than any I have heard so far. (*She looks at the walls of the hut*) Adam?

ADAM What?

EVE What made you pick brown?

ADAM Because wood is brown.

EVE (*She rises. The end of this speech will be drowned out by a rising swell of musical "rain"*) But berries are red. We could squeeze some berries against the wood, and make it nice and colorful . . . not all over, just from here to here. We'll leave a border on top and bottom . . . and on that wall, some shells, I think. Have you thought of hanging grass in the doorway?

(*The lights fade out as* ADAM *holds his head at her torrent of words. After a pause, the lights restore and we see a completely redecorated hut, just as* EVE *had envisioned it.* ADAM *is standing in front of the hut, a basket of melons in his hand. He turns to the audience and pantomimes "See—see what I mean?" He sits on the tub at the left of the hut and thumps a melon, listening for its hollowness. He keeps looking back at the hut and finally talks to the audience. The music has vamped throughout*)

ADAM Sunday, June ninth. (*Singing*)

She keeps filling up the hut with rubbish,
Like flowers
And plants.
And not only is it overcrowded—
It's loaded
With ants.
She is definitely too intrusive,
A nuisance,
And yet . . .
She's an interesting creature—
This Eve.

She's developing a strange new habit
Which doesn't
Make sense.
She's forever reaching out to touch me,
Which makes me
Feel tense.
She is definitely quite eccentric,
A numskull,
And yet . . .
She's an interesting creature—
This Eve.

Colors drive her absolutely crazy
The gold of the sun,
The purple of the hills,
Crimson-colored clouds in the skies.
When I say this is sentimental hogwash,
Foolishness,
She simply sighs.

THE APPLE TREE

When I'd rather be alone and resting,
Then she comes
Around,
And invariably starts describing
Some wonder
She's found.
She invariably gets my back up,
Yet invariably I perceive
She's an interesting creature—
This Eve.

Once I saw her standing on a hilltop
Her head tilted back,
The sunlight on her face
Gazing at the flight of a bird;
And suddenly I saw that she was—
Beautiful—
Beautiful, yes, that's the word.

There are animals around this garden
More soothing
Than she,
But there's nothing in the whole of Eden
More pleasant
To see.
If she'd only learn to keep her mouth shut
One minute at a time,
Why, I believe
I could possibly enjoy
Just watching
This curiously interesting creature—
Called Eve.

(On the last word of the song he slowly moves

back to the tub and sits deep in thought and confusion. EVE *enters, wearing a mad hat made of flowers. He quickly picks up a melon and goes back to his thumping)*

EVE Adam, I just had a wonderful idea.

ADAM *(Indicating her hat with distaste)* Is that it?

EVE *(Puts her basket in hut)* No. What I thought . . . *(Turns to him)* Do you like it?

ADAM I think it's unbecoming and ridiculous. And I want you to take it off this instant.

EVE *(She does)* I thought it would please you.

ADAM How could it please me to see you walking around covered with rubbish?

EVE Rubbish? Flowers, rubbish? These beautiful creatures that catch the smile of God out of the sky and preserve it? Rubbish? Does everything have to be useful? Isn't there anything you care about except thumping those melons? We've been given a world full of wonderful secrets and mysteries. There's so much to learn! Oh, Adam, to see everything and to know everything . . . why, that might take us weeks! How can you be so narrow?

ADAM I have a lot of interests. It may surprise you to learn that only yesterday I invented something brand new.

EVE Oh, Adam, what?

ADAM (*Rises*) Humor.

EVE Humor?

ADAM Does that word puzzle you? I thought it might. I'll be happy to explain. Yesterday, I was sitting beside the path that leads to the cornfield and I happened to notice this yellow clucker . . .

EVE Chicken.

ADAM All right!

EVE It looks like . . .

ADAM All right! Have it your way! I happened to notice this chicken. For a long time it walked slowly back and forth, hesitating, and then suddenly it zipped across the path. And I thought to myself, "Why did that chicken cross that path?" And then I thought, "To get to the other side!" (*He is hysterical and falls about, finally reaching up to her*) That's the world's first joke. And I made it up. Don't you see the humor of it? (EVE *has been growing increasingly puzzled by this whole thing. She obliges* ADAM *with a smile but shrugs apologetically*) I guess you had to be there . . . and I'm going there.

(*He turns and starts to leave*)

EVE Adam, don't you want to hear my wonderful idea?

ADAM No.

EVE Oh, Adam . . .

ADAM *(He goes back to her)* Well, what is it?

EVE I've been thinking . . . we're different from anything else on earth. And our home should be different.

ADAM I thought it was.

EVE And today I had the feeling that the grass around our hut should be different from all other grass.

ADAM Different how?

EVE Shorter.

ADAM How could it be shorter—unless it was cut?
(As ADAM *and* EVE *stare at one another, the lights fade. When they come up again,* EVE *is gone and* ADAM *is alone)*

ADAM *(He sits on the wooden tub)* Monday, June tenth. Note: I finally discovered the purpose of the week. To rest up from Sunday. This relentless pursuit of improvements is making me feel more hampered than ever. What's truly puzzling is that the more time we spend together, the closer we get; and the closer we get, the more anxious it makes me. Anyway, there's one bright spot. She's taken up with a snake now. I'm glad, because the snake talks and this allows me a little time to rest. Eve has also taken to spending a great deal of time at the pond. I don't know why.
(The lights fade on ADAM, *who exits, and come up*

on EVE, *looking at herself in the pond and making up her face with petals)*

EVE *(Singing)*
Look at you,
Look at me,
How much more alike could
Two girls be?
Here we stand,
Sisters and
Friends.

When I speak
You speak too,
And when I am silent
So are you.
That's the test
Of two best
Friends.

When my life is hard to bear,
Then I run to see you there,
And
My heart blooms,
Your face beams,
Nothing is as awful
As it seems.
We're such dear . . .
More than mere . . .
Friends.

(The lights fade on EVE *and come up on* ADAM. *He's sitting on a tub)*

ADAM (*Laughing*) Eve fell in the pond yesterday. She damn near strangled. She said it was so cold and uncomfortable in there that she felt sorry for the fish. So last night she got a lot of them out and brought them inside. And she put them in my bed to keep warm.

EVE (*Rises and crosses to* ADAM) Hello, Adam.

ADAM Eve, tonight those fish go back to the pond.

EVE But it's so uncomfortable there!

ADAM Eve, I've been watching those fish off and on all morning, and I don't see that they're any happier than they were before. They're just . . . quieter.

EVE But . . .

ADAM I don't want 'em in my bed. They're clammy!

EVE But, Adam . . .

ADAM (*Rises*) I want you to put 'em back! Do you understand me?

EVE Yes, Adam.

ADAM All right then.
(*He picks up his tub and starts to leave*)

EVE Where are you going?

ADAM (*Stopping*) Somewhere I can be by myself.

EVE Where?

ADAM Over the falls.

EVE Not in that leaky tub? Oh, Adam, I wish you wouldn't!

ADAM Eve, this has nothing to do with you!

EVE It makes me shudder! It's not safe.

ADAM Well, I like it. It's cool. And I like the plunge.

EVE Please, don't. Not in the tub. You can't imagine how it frightens me. I can't bear it.

(She tries to grab the tub. He pulls it away from her)

ADAM You can't? Well, I can't bear this everlasting complaining. First, you complained about my going over the falls in a barrel. So I made a tub. Did that satisfy you? No, sir. Now you complain about the tub! And if it isn't the tub it'll be something else. Eve, I won't have it. I don't want to be complained at, I don't want to be clucked over, I don't want to be clung to. I'm going to the falls, and after that I'm not sure where I'm going. So don't wait for me.

(He storms off. She yells after him)

EVE Adam, would you bring back some of those hollyhocks that grow by the falls?

ADAM *(Offstage)* I hate flowers!

(EVE *goes back to the pond; her mood is a mixture of heartache, petulance, and pride.*)

EVE (*Singing*)

And on days when he withdraws,
I'm less lonely now because
If
I should need sympathy,
You would never turn your
Back on me.
I have you.
Who needs two
Friends?

(*The* SNAKE, *in tuxedo, smoking a pipe, enters behind* EVE. *He throws a pipe cleaner into the pond, making the reflection shatter*)

Wait! Don't go away!

SNAKE There's no one there, Eve.

(EVE *whirls, startled*)

EVE What? Oh, hello, Snake.

SNAKE I said, there's no one there.

EVE There is so! My friend's there. And she'll be back.

SNAKE No, Eve. That's what's called a reflection. (*He kneels down*) You see, when waves of one kind traveling in one medium arrive at another in which their velocity is different, part of their energy is turned back into the first medium. In this case, the waves are light rays which appear to come from a literally inverted replica of the luminous source, and it is this image which is then focused on the retina.

EVE I don't believe you.

SNAKE Well, it's so. Look . . . (*He leans over* EVE *and wiggles his arms and legs.* EVE *compares the reflection with the* SNAKE) See. That's not my brother. That's me.

EVE Then I have no one! No friend! Nothing!

SNAKE (*Leaning back*) What about Adam?

EVE (*Turning, lying across his lap*) He doesn't even like me! He thinks I'm a numskull. And I am . . . so how could he like me! Oh, I wish I was educated—like you.

SNAKE Would you really like that?

EVE Oh, yes!

SNAKE Nothing could be simpler.

EVE How? How?

SNAKE You know that apple tree on the other side of the hill?

EVE Forbidden fruit?

SNAKE Who says?

EVE Adam.

SNAKE My dear girl, the forbidden fruit in this garden is hardly apples. It's chestnuts.

EVE Chestnuts?

SNAKE Well, not literally. When I say "chestnuts," that's a figurative term meaning old and moldy jokes.

EVE The thing Adam calls humor.

SNAKE Exactly. There's your forbidden fruit.

EVE (*Rising*) Chestnuts! I didn't know that. See how ignorant I am.

(*The music starts. The* SNAKE *holds up his hand, freezing* EVE *in her tracks*)

SNAKE (*Singing*)

Listen closely. Let me fill you in
About the rich, ripe, round, red,
Rosy apples they call forbidden fruit.
What I'm about to say is
Confidential, so promise you'll be mute.
Because if every creature in the garden knows,
They'll come 'round like hungry buffalos,
And in no time there'll be none of those
Precious apples left for you and me.

Now, in the average apple
You're accustomed to skin, seeds, flesh, and core.
But you will find that these are
Special apples that give you something more.
Why, every seed contains some information you

Need to speed your education; the
Seeds, indeed, of all creation are here.
Why, be foolish, my dear,
Come with me
To that tree.

EVE I don't think Adam would approve. Maybe they're not forbidden, but I still have qualms.

SNAKE (*Singing*)
With every sweet and juicy
Luscious bite of this not forbidden fruit,
You'll see your mind expand and
Your perceptions grow more and more acute.

And you can teach him plumbing and philosophy,
New techniques for glazing pottery,
Wood-craft, first-aid, home economy,
Madam, Adam will be overjoyed!

When he becomes aware of
Your attainments he'll beam with loving pride
And he will say,
(*Holding her in his arms*)
"O, Eve, you're
Indispensable! Please, don't leave my side!"
And with your nifty, new-found education, he'll
Relish every conversation; why
(*Moving around her*)
You'll be Adam's inspiration this way!
Just an apple a day.
Wait and see.

Come with me
To that tree!
Now!

(He takes her arm and pulls her offstage. The lights fade; when they come up again, ADAM *is seated tranquilly on his tub, drying himself with a towel. He is singing as if he is in the shower)*

ADAM *(Singing)*

I see animals and birds and flowers,
Every color, every shape and size.
Moss and pebbles and a host of wonders
Gleaming everywhere I aim my eyes.
So if ever I'm attacked by boredom,
I'll just open up my eyes and see
This diversified, curious, fascinating, bountiful,
Beautiful, beautiful world,
I love.

(He laughs and suddenly freezes. He calls out in alarm)

Hey—hey—you there, growler—I mean, lion. Leave that lamb alone. Don't do that, you'll hurt him. I said stop that! What do you think you're doing? Stop it! Stop it! *(He steps back in horror)* Oh, my God! Oh, my God! *(He looks about in anguish as the stage darkens)* Oh, my God!

(Thunder is heard rolling down ominously)

EVE *(Entering, she throws her arms around* ADAM *in fear. She is carrying an apple, though we don't see it as yet. She wears a robe of flowers)* There you are— Oh, Adam!

ADAM You did it! You did it! I warned you. You ate the apples, didn't you? The forbidden fruit! Do you know what you did? I told you. I said don't touch that fruit—something terrible would happen. And now death has come into the garden. (*He has pushed her away and now throws his towel to the ground*) How could you do it? How could you do such a damnable thing?

EVE I didn't do it! I mean, it wasn't the apples—they're not forbidden.

ADAM No? Then what is?

EVE Chestnuts.

ADAM Chestnuts? Where the hell did you pick that up?

EVE The snake told me. And he knows everything. In fact, this whole thing is probably your fault.

ADAM My fault? I didn't eat any chestnuts.

EVE Not that kind. This kind of chestnut is a joke. Have you been making up jokes, Adam? Tell the truth.

ADAM I did think of one . . . (*She reacts audibly and turns away*) but I didn't say it out loud! Oh, my . . . I was standing here—just before it all happened—and I was thinking about the falls. And I thought, "How wonderful it is to see that vast body of water tumble down there." And then I thought, "Yes, but it would be a lot more wonderful to see it tumble up!"

EVE That's it. That's what did it.

ADAM Oh, my. Oh my, oh my. . . . (*To heaven*) Why was I born so witty?

EVE We have to leave the garden, don't we?

ADAM We broke the rule . . . *I* broke the rule. I'm sorry, Eve.

EVE Oh . . . you didn't know.

(*They embrace.* ADAM *suddenly notices* EVE'S *costume*)

ADAM Eve, you know I can't stand to see you wearing that rubbish. Please take it off.

(*He makes a gesture to help her off with her robe. To his surprise she resists, with some embarrassment*)

EVE No, don't do that. You mustn't. Please, Adam. No, don't please!

ADAM You're behaving like an idiot. If you want to make a silly spectacle of yourself, go right ahead. I know what I'm going to do. I haven't eaten all day.

EVE (*Showing it to him*) Would you like an apple?

ADAM Oh, it's one of those.

EVE They're not forbidden.

ADAM I know, but somehow it still goes against my principles. (*Takes the apple*) It's certainly a fine looking specimen, isn't it? Considering the lateness of the season and all. I guess principles have no real force unless you're well fed. (*He takes a bite and chews it for a moment. He reaches down and picks up his towel*) Turn your back. Don't you have any modesty at all?

(*He wraps himself in the towel*)

EVE Sorry. (*She turns her back*) Adam?

ADAM What?

EVE (*Starting to cry*) It looks like rain.

ADAM I know. Come on. We'll have to build a new shelter somewhere.

(*They exit, as Eden flys out. A platform rolls out with a rail on one end and a bench in the middle of it. It is night*)

ADAM (*Enters onto the porch, corn-cob pipe in hand, contentedly puffing as he sits on the bench. He picks up a piece of hickory twig and a knife and slowly whittles*) Eve calls this place Tonawanda. You know, it *looks* like Tonawanda. I find she's a good deal of a companion. I can see I'd be lonesome and depressed without her, now that I've lost my property.

EVE (*Entering onto the porch with a rough wool sweater which she throws over* ADAM*'s shoulders. Giving him* *a quick hug, she talks from behind him)* Did you like the baked apples?

(She picks up a watering can and gardens)

ADAM Very tasty.

EVE I like to try new things.

ADAM I remember when you invented fire. I never thought it would be practical.

EVE That reminds me—how's the multiplication table coming?

ADAM I don't know. I get as far as five times nine is twenty-seven and the whole thing goes to pieces.

EVE You'll get it, dear.

ADAM *(With a cough)* Well, I'm tired.

(He stands and gazes down at her. She puts the can down, stops weeding, and joins him on the porch)

EVE It's late.

ADAM *(His arm about her waist)* Eve, is it my imagination or have you been putting on weight?

(The lights fade out as they exit. The music to "It's a Fish" begins and the lights restore)

ADAM *(Entering hurriedly from the house onto the porch. He paces back and forth)* I just got back from a hunting trip up North and found that Eve had caught some new kind of animal. (*Singing*)

Now I could swear
That it's a fish,
Tho' it resembles us in every way but size.

She gives it milk,
And every night
She picks it up and pats and pets it when it cries.

I always knew
She pitied fish,
But it's ridiculous to make them household pets.

She says it's not a fish.
I say it is a fish
'Cause it surrounds itself with water
Almost every chance it gets.

(EVE *enters from the cabin into the porch carrying a bundle wrapped in a rough wool blanket, and acting very wary of* ADAM)

ADAM Why won't you let me put it in the pond?

EVE I told you it's not a fish!

ADAM How will we ever find out what it is, if we don't experiment?

EVE I don't *care* what it is! (*Her voice rises to a frenzied scream*) You keep away from it!

ADAM You're standing in the way of science. (*She takes*

the bundle into the cabin. He follows her into the cabin; a beat later he backs out. He sings)

It's not a fish.
Fish never scream,
And this one does, tho' on occasion it says "Goo."

Its legs are long,
Its arms are short,
So I suspect that it's a kind of kangaroo.

And since it came
I pity Eve,
She's gotten madder by the minute, and it shows.

Just now I said to her
That I would much prefer
To have it stuffed for my collection,
And she punched me in the nose!

(The music to "Go to Sleep Whatever You Are" begins. EVE *comes on carrying the bundle and looks around to see if she is alone. She sits on the porch rail)*

EVE *(Singing)*

Go to sleep, whatever you are,
Lay your head on my breast.

Close your eyes and open your paws,
You need plenty of rest

Doesn't faze me
If you grow up to be
Pony or poodle or sheep.

You're my own, whatever you are.
Sleep . . . sleep . . . sleep.

(EVE *goes in the house.* ADAM *re-enters*)

ADAM (*Singing*)

It's growing teeth,
And it can bite,
And I'm convinced that what we have here is a bear.

I'm worried sick,
But Eve is not.
She burned the muzzle that I made for it to wear.

I've searched the woods,
I've baited traps,
And yet I couldn't find its sister or its brother.
And tho' I've hunted far and wide
While Eve has hardly stepped outside,
I'll be damned if she didn't catch another!

(*Blackout. The lights focus on* EVE *on the porch bench. She is snapping beans in a wooden bowl*)

EVE They are boys. We found that out long ago. It was their coming in that small, immature shape that puzzled us. (*Yells offstage*) Cain! Abel! Keep out of my garden! You'll ruin the flowers! The old garden. That seems like a dream to me. It was beautiful. Surpassingly beautiful. But still a dream. Making supper for three hungry males is not a dream.

(*The lights fade on* EVE *and come up on* ADAM, *who has a stylized plow and a rake*)

ADAM They're nearly as big as I am now. Abel is a good

boy. But if Cain had stayed a bear it would have improved him. I never know what's coming next. A fire started for spite; a creature killed without sense or reason. I have come to depend on Eve more than I would have believed possible. I used to think she talked too much. But now I'd be sorry to have that voice fall silent and pass out of my life.

(The lights fade on ADAM; *they come up on* EVE, *who is sewing a sweater)*

EVE Some time back, my boys were fighting. And Cain struck Abel and ran away. Now Cain is gone, and Abel's dead. There is too much stillness in the house.

ADAM *(Enters, carrying the rake)* Are you all right?

EVE *(Still sewing)* Yes. Adam, I've been thinking. I hope that when we die, we die together.

ADAM *(He puts his hand on her shoulder)* That's a subject, I'd—

EVE Wait. If one of us must go first, my prayer is that I'm the one.

ADAM I don't want to—

EVE You're strong, and I'm weak. You're more necessary to me than I am to you.

ADAM That's not true.

EVE Yes, it's true. It's always been true.

ADAM (*Changing the subject*) Listen, listen—I've got a good one for you. Why do I always wear brown suspenders?

EVE (*Laughing heartily*) That's my favorite.
(*Still laughing*)

ADAM (*Beginning to laugh*) Oh, I forgot . . .
(*He laughs, coughs a bit and exits, the rake over his shoulder*)

EVE (*Gazing after him and chuckling*) Life without him would not be life—I don't think I could endure it. And yet, if I ask myself why I love him, I find I don't know. It's not on account of his gracious and considerate ways—he's a bit flawed in those respects. I love certain birds because of their song, but that hardly applies to Adam. (*Music begins and she sings*)

What makes me love him?
It's not his singing.
I've heard his singing:
It sours the milk.
And yet, it's gotten to the point
Where I prefer that kind of milk.

What makes me love him?
It's not his learning.
He's learned so slowly
His whole life long.
And tho' he really knows
A multitude of things, they're mostly wrong.

He is a good man,
Yet I would love him
If he abused me
Or used me ill.

And tho' he's handsome,
I know inside me
Were he a plain man,
I'd love him still.

What makes me love him?
It's quite beyond me.
It must be something
I can't define;
Unless it's merely that he's masculine,
And that he's mine.

(EVE *slowly gathers up the sweater and the bowl of beans. Feeling the chill of the night, she rises and exits into the house*)

ADAM (*Entering and bearing a great sadness*) Eve died today. I knew she would, of course. Well, at least her prayer was answered—she went first. Now that she's gone, I realize something I didn't realize before. I used to think it was a terrible tragedy when Eve and I had to leave the garden. Now I know it really didn't matter. Because, wheresoever she was, there was Eden. (*The lights pick up the flowerbed area*) And now, I have to go water her flowers. She loved them, you know.

(*The strains of "Here in Eden" are heard as* ADAM *picks up the watering can and tends the flowers. After a bit, he wipes his brow and bends down and weeds*)

Curtain

PART II

The Lady or the Tiger?

Based on *The Lady or the Tiger?*
by Frank R. Stockton

At the rise of the curtain, the performer who has played SNAKE *in "The Diary of Adam and Eve" enters alone, crosses, and sings, accompanying himself on a guitar.*

BALLADEER (*Singing*)

I'll tell you a truth
That's hard to swallow;
I'll tell you a truth,
Oh, listen well.
If you are in love
With a lover who's jealous,
Then sooner or later
You're headed for hell.

So say good-bye
And don't you wait,
Because tomorrow
May be too late.
Yes, listen well
To what I say,
Tell jealous lovers
To go away.

I'll tell you a tale
For you to ponder,
I'll tell you a tale
Oh, listen well.
A curious tale,
It tells of a Princess,
And it tells of her lover
And all that befell.

(The orchestra begins to play a savage rhythm) It happened a long time ago in a far-away kingdom, ruled by an absolute monarch, King Arik. This King had a daughter, the Princess Barbara, and a more hot-blooded, high-handed pair never lived.

(As the BALLADEER *finishes, the lights suddenly come on full. The* BALLADEER *exits as the Guards appear snapping whips.* KING ARIK'S *procession is barbaric and splendid. His throne and the throne of* PRINCESS BARBARA *are quite impressive and quite high)*

KING'S MEN *(Singing)*

Make way!
He comes!
His Royal Tallness!
His Highest Highness!
His Way, Way Upness!
His Mountainship!
Make way!
He comes!
King Arik!

(The KING'S *throne enters and moves into position with the* KING *and his male retinue;* PRINCESS BARBARA *enters with handmaidens)*

HANDMAIDENS *(Singing)*

Make way!
She comes!
Her Regal Proudness!
Her Flashing Eye-ness!
Her Self-Indulgeness!
Her Goddessness!

Make way!
She comes!
Princess Barbara!

(As the procession ends and PRINCESS BARBARA'S *throne turns into position, the lights black out. A spot picks up the* BALLADEER*)*

BALLADEER Now, this King was something of an idealist on the subject of justice, and so he invented a legal system which he believed absolutely guaranteed every prisoner a fair trial. It worked this way. All trials were held in a large arena. *(Lighting makes the center of the stage an arena)* In this arena there were two doors. They stood side by side and looked exactly alike. *(A wall with two rather large, primitive doors appears)* The prisoner had his choice. *(The* PRISONER *is brought from the bleachers and looks apprehensively at the* KING*)* He could open either door, but he knew that behind one of them there was a ferocious and ravenous tiger!

(The Guards hurl the PRISONER *to the floor and return to their places on bleachers on either side of the arena doors, where the court has taken their places)*

KING *(Singing)*
Pris'ner
Choose!
It's your chance to prove
Your innocence or guilt!

ALL *(Singing)*
Salute!
Yeh yeh manna!

Yeh yeh callu!
Yeh yeh manna callu
Yeh yeh!

(During the preceding chant, everyone gives the prisoner the ritual salute. They point one arm heavenward and the other earthward, symbolizing the alternate outcomes of the two choices. Then they put a hand over each eye, symbolizing the blindness of chance. When this ceremony is over, the prisoner makes an elaborate bow to the KING *and to the* PRINCESS. *Then he faces upstage and goes to the two doors. He can't decide which to choose. The crowd reacts vocally as the prisoner reaches for the door on their side of the arena. He is confused and turns front in abject confusion. Finally in desperation he chooses one door and opens it. The tiger leaps at his throat. He screams, he tries to run, he falls, kicks, and finally lies quiet)*

ALL *(During the above, singing)*
Ai, ai!
Ai, ai!
That one so young and fair should die!
Ai, ee!
Ai, ee!
A terrifying sight to see
(The PRISONER *is dead)*
But better him than me!
Yeh!
(Everyone on the stage freezes)

BALLADEER However, suppose he had chosen the other

door . . . (*The underscoring of the previous scene is played backward. The previous movements are played backward up to the moment where the prisoner makes his choice*) Why then a beautiful lady came out and he married her on the spot—whether he wanted to or not.

(*To the accompaniment of the chant the* PRISONER *with his* BRIDE *dance down to the* KING, *who marries them instantly*)

ALL

Ai, ee! Ai, ee!
A gratifying sight to see
Ai, ai! Ai, ai!

GIRLS (*Singing*)

A wedding always makes me cry!

MEN (*Singing*)

But better he than I! Yeh!

(*The lights black out*)

BALLADEER (*In a spotlight*) And this was the simple and beautiful system of justice in King Arik's kingdom. If you happened to choose the lady, you were obviously innocent; if you happened to choose the tiger, you were just as obviously guilty. And no one could deny that it was a fair trial, because the choice lay in the prisoner's own hands. (*The palace set has come into view and the lights come up gradually*) Now. There was also in this kingdom a soldier of exceptional bravery, and his name was Captain Sanjar!

(*The* BALLADEER *exits. The court is in attendance around the thrones. A* GUARD *on top of the stairs, which lead through the palace arch, salutes the* KING)

GUARD Your Mountainship, Captain Sanjar of your Royal Camels has just returned from the battlefield.

BARBARA (*In great surprise*) Oh!

KING (*With a gesture*) In!

GUARD In!

OFFSTAGE VOICE In!

(*A gong sounds.* SANJAR *enters in primitive battle garb, helmet in hand. He is tired and tattered*)

SANJAR (*Kneels in salute at the top of the stairs*) We won!

(*The court cheers.* SANJAR *collapses and rolls down the stairs, unconscious*)

KING (*Ignoring* SANJAR, *he rises*) Victory is ours! (*There is a fanfare; the* KING *climbs down the throne*) We pray now. To the altar.

(*All rise and follow the* KING *up the stairs*)

ALL (*Singing*)
Victory is ours,
Victory is ours,
Victory is ours . . .

(*The singing and the music fade as they all exit.* BARBARA *is the last to go out.* NADJIRA *has remained behind and now kneels by the prone* SANJAR. *She takes out a kerchief and wipes* SANJAR'S *brow tenderly. A gong sounds.* BARBARA *returns through the feather curtain and sees* NADJIRA *embracing* SANJAR)

BARBARA Nadjira, pray go. (NADJIRA *does not move*) Nadjira, go pray. Get out.

(NADJIRA *slowly rises, genuflects to* BARBARA, *and exits, backwards.* BARBARA, *left alone, checks through the curtain that no one is spying and goes to* SANJAR. *She kneels next to him and kisses his brow*)

SANJAR (*Waking, he rises to his knees and embraces* BARBARA) Barbara!

BARBARA Sanjar! (*Holding his face in her hands*) Sanjar!

SANJAR Bar . . .

BARBARA Shh! Someone's coming!

(*She leaps away from him*)

SANJAR (*Assuming the "salute" position, he gives his report to* BARBARA. *A* GUARD, *carrying an urn, enters and exits*) . . . three killed, seventeen wounded, but we slashed them to ribbons, your Proudness. The next day . . .

BARBARA (*Watching the* GUARD *leave*) They deserved every slash! Tell me more, Captain, more! (*The* GUARD *exits; she turns to* SANJAR) Do you love me?

SANJAR Forever!

BARBARA Did you miss me?

SANJAR Did I ever! (*The music to "Forbidden Love" begins.* SANJAR *sings*)

When battle had all but drained me,
One vision alone sustained me,
The thought of you
And our forbidden love.

BARBARA (*Singing*)

Whenever my days were harried
And father would say "Get married,"
I thought of you
And our forbidden love.

(*They move away from each other, checking to see if they are alone*)

SANJAR (*Singing*)

So kiss me, come kiss me,
For who knows when
We may kiss like this
Aga . . .

BARBARA Shh! Someone's coming.

(*Two* HANDMAIDENS *enter and exit.* SANJAR *is back in his "salute" position.* BARBARA *is pacing about*)

SANJAR That day we killed all their camels, two corporals, and I suffered a small wound in the head, your Proudness.

BARBARA Don't bore me with your injuries, Captain. Describe the slaughter. More details, I relish details!

(The HANDMAIDENS *are gone; she turns to* SANJAR *again; he rises)*

SANJAR Barbara, this is torture!

BARBARA I know.

SANJAR Let's run away.

BARBARA Where?

SANJAR I have this cousin who served with Julius Caesar, and he told me about a place called Gaul.

BARBARA *(Looking around, distractedly)* What?

SANJAR Gaul. *(The music to "In Gaul" begins.* SANJAR *sings)*

They tell me it's divided in three parts.
We'll pick the part that's closest to our hearts.

(He puts his arms around her waist. They gaze forward)

In Gaul
We'd live so simply,
No more feathers and fuss,
Just the children and us.

In Gaul
We'd have a garden
On the outskirts of town,
And a house painted brown.

BARBARA Why brown?

SANJAR (*Singing*)
No more stolen kisses

BARBARA (*Turns to him, singing*)
No more stolen sighs

SANJAR (*Turns to her*)
Stolen nights

BARBARA (*She takes a step toward him*)
Stolen days

SANJAR
Stolen bites

BARBARA
Swollen eyes

BOTH (*In an embrace, as before*)
In Gaul
We'd be so happy.

BARBARA
Oh, Sanjar, my hawk!

SANJAR
Barbara, my dove!

BOTH
We'd be two ordinary
People in love,

In love
In Gaul.

BARBARA It's impossible! (*Turns to him and sings*)
You know as well as I our place is here.
My people need me

SANJAR (*Bitterly, singing*)
And I have my career.

BOTH (*Turning to each other. They hold hands and sing*)
Tho' this is our fate, we'll fight it.
Our passion will thrive despite it.
And tho' we're at odds
With all the gods above,
We'll keep well hidden
Our forbidden love!
(*They embrace. A gong sounds.* KING ARIK *enters at the top of the stairs, glaring down at them. Two Guards are behind him.* BARBARA *crosses;* SANJAR *kneels in salute*)

KING (*On the steps, singing*)
Barbara!
How could you!

BARBARA (*Singing*)
I love him!

KING
Forbidden!

SANJAR
King Arik . . .

KING

Be silent!

BARBARA

Oh, Daddy!

KING (*Sings to* BARBARA)

You know and I know
The sacred commandment:
For a common man
To make love to you
Is a sin against
The gods!

(*He points to* SANJAR *and commands the Guards*)

Take him!

(*The Guards seize* SANJAR. *They exit*)

BARBARA What are you going to do to him?

KING He will have a fair trial.

(*He exits*)

BARBARA (*Left alone as the lights fade, leaving her in a spot*) A trial! The tiger! (*Singing*)

Those razor teeth,
Those iron claws,
His handsome throat
Between those jaws.
Not my Sanjar.
Lying there!
Dying there!
I'll stop that
If it's the last thing . . .

But how? Others have tried. No one has ever been able to discover, before the trial, which door hides the tiger. Someone must know. But who? (*The lights reveal the* BALLADEER, *in tiger-keeper hat and whip, leaning on the portal*) The Royal Tiger-keeper, of course! (*She crosses slowly to him. He kneels as she approaches*) You must help me!

(*The music to "Forbidden Fruit" begins as the palace set flies out.* BARBARA *removes her jewelry, which she offers the* BALLADEER *during the ensuing song*)

BALLADEER (*Singing*)
I must advise your Proudness
There are things it is better
Not to know . . .

BARBARA I don't need your advice!

BALLADEER
If you insist, your Proudness,
Then of course I will tell you even so . . .

BARBARA Good!

BALLADEER
You will not reconsider?

BARBARA No.

BALLADEER
You are certain you want this knowledge?

BARBARA Yes.

BALLADEER
Though I warn you against this knowledge?

BARBARA Which door!

BALLADEER
Be it on your own head!
(He rises, close to her)
What's forbidden to know
You shall know.
Be it so . . .
(He whispers in her ear and exits)

BARBARA I've got it! Oh, Sanjar, I've got it! *(She sings)*
I've got what you want,
I've got what you need.
I know how much you want it.
Yeh! Yeh! Sanjar.

I know my father would kill me
If he knew
My heart was set on giving
What I've got to you. Yeh! Yeh!

I know what I know.
You need what I know.
What's mine is yours,
You know it. Yeh! Yeh! Sanjar!
If we don't share this secret
You just might die,
So I will give it to you,
And when I give it to you,
You'll shout for joy
And so will I!

Yes, I will give it to you,
And when I give it to you,
You'll shout for joy
And so will I!

(She closes her cape, glowing in victory, and does not hear the procession entering. Guards are bearing a resplendent NADJIRA *on an open palanquin.* BARBARA *finally sees them)*

Nadjira? *(The procession never stops.* NADJIRA *is quietly singing "I've Got What You Want" in obvious anticipation)* Nadjira? Guard! *(To the Guard bringing up the rear)* Guard! Where are you taking my servant?

GUARD To the arena, your Proudness. The King has chosen Nadjira to wait behind the second door.

BARBARA Nadjira! The other door! Of course! *(Calling after them as they exit)* I forbid it! I forbid it! I forbid it! *(They are gone. She looks after them. The lights change to a blue glow.* BARBARA *slowly faces front. The* BALLADEER *enters pushing a tiger cage and grinning.* BARBARA *looks at him, then at the litter. When she meets the cage she suddenly whirls her cape and sings)*

Tiger, tiger,
Put on your napkin,
Someone is coming to dine.
Tiger, tiger,
You do the carving,
Your claws are sharper than mine.

(She climbs onto the cage)

Slash him with your teeth,
Smash him with your paws,
Bite him again, bite him again,
Harder! Harder!

Tear him into bits!
Rip him into shreds!
Slice him into ruby ribbons!
Tiger, tiger,
I hope you're hungry
(She gets off the cage)
I'll cheer you on from the stands.
(The BALLADEER *exits with the cage. The lights fade, leaving* BARBARA *in a spot)*
Sanjar, Sanjar,
What am I saying?
I'd have your blood on my hands!
Your dying screams
Haunting my dreams
Ai!
Ai!

I don't want him dead,
Better dead than wed.
Nobody else, nobody else
Gets you, Sanjar!
How can I decide?
Burial or bride?
Ai! The lady or the tiger?

Lady? Tiger?
Each way is torture.
Each way I'm still on the rack.
Sanjar, Sanjar,
Each way I lose you,
Each way is hopelessly black.
How can I choose?
Each way I lose?
(She begins to exit)

Ai!! . . . Ai!! . . . Ai!! . . . Ai!! . . .

(As BARBARA *exits the music blends into the procession and the court enters bearing the thrones into the arena.* SANJAR *is led by two Guards)*

MEN *(Singing)*	LADIES *(Singing)*
Make way!	Make way!
He comes!	She comes!
His Royal Tallness!	Her Regal Proudness!
His Highest Highness!	Her Flashing Eye-ness!
His Way, Way Upness!	Her Self-Indulgeness!
His Mountainship!	Her Goddessness!
Make way!	Make way!
He comes!	She comes!
King Arik!	Princess Barbara!

(The orchestra vamps as the court proceeds to their places in the arena bleachers, leaving a lone SANJAR *on his knees. The music continues throughout)*

KING *(Pointing down from the throne, singing)*

Pris'ner, choose!
It's your chance to prove your innocence or guilt!

(The court silently pantomimes the ritual salute as the lights fade to black, with a spot on SANJAR*)*

SANJAR Barbara, I know you know which door is which. I saw it in your eyes. Give me a sign. A sign! *(Singing)*

Which door should I choose?
Left? Right? Left? Right?
Show me . . . Guide me . . .
Barbara, Barbara,
I know you are my only hope.

(The spot leaves SANJAR *and picks up* BARBARA *on her throne)*

BARBARA *(Singing)*

Which door should I choose?
Left? Right? Left? Right?
Torment! Torture!
The lady, the tiger?
Sanjar! Sanjar!
This choice is tearing me apart!

(She eats grapes. The spot picks up the KING *and slowly the entire court, as they join the song)*

KING and CHORUS *(Singing in canon)*

Which door will he choose?
Left? Right? Left? Right?
Dead man? Wed man?
The lady, the tiger?
This door? That door?
Which door will he choose?

(The entire court does the ritual incantation and sings)

Yeh, yeh, manna,
Yeh, yeh, callu
Yeh, yeh, manna callu
Yeh, yeh.

(The lights black out. Spots remain on BARBARA *and* SANJAR. BARBARA*'s hands slowly uncover her eyes. With agonizing deliberateness she reaches a decision and finally points to a door. The music builds in suspense as* SANJAR *rises. After a long look at* BARBARA, *he reaches for a door. The entire action freezes)*

BALLADEER (*Entering behind the* KING'*s throne*)

Before we go on
Let's look at the problem:
The lady, or tiger
Which will come out?
The deeper we probe
The heart of Barbara
The more we discover
The outcome's in doubt.

If you have loved,
You understand
How love and hate can
Walk hand in hand.
So place yourself
In Barbara's shoes:
The lady or the tiger,
Which did she choose?

(*The* BALLADEER *exits. The freeze picture remains as the curtain slowly falls, with only* BARBARA *in a spotlight*)

Curtain

PART III

Passionella

Based on *Passionella*
by Jules Feiffer

Barbara Harris as PASSIONELLA.

The lights come up on a rooftop, showing the New York skyline in the distance. ELLA *is energetically sweeping a chimney, accompanied by brisk, cheerful music. The music stops abruptly;* ELLA *freezes.*

NARRATOR Ella was a chimney-sweep. (*The music resumes and* ELLA *works; the music stops and she freezes*) She worked in a big office building downtown. (*The music resumes and* ELLA *works. The music stops and* ELLA *climbs down from the chimney on a ladder*) But it wasn't what she really wanted to do.

(*The music to "Oh, to Be a Movie Star" begins*)

ELLA (*To the audience*) Oh, no, I'm only doing this to make a living.

NARRATOR As she often tried to tell people . . .

ELLA (*Singing*)

Chimneys are cozy,
Chimneys are warm.
I think of chimneys
As ports in a storm.
But warm and cozy or not,
I would give up the lot
If I could only be a movie star.

A movie star.
Oh, to be a movie star,
A beautiful, glamorous movie star.

(ELLA *does several bars of a clumsy soft-shoe dance*)

No one imagines
I harbor this hope.
People who know me
Keep sending me soap;
They see soot-stains and tar.
They'd see how wrong they are
If I could only be a movie star.

A movie star,
Oh, to be a movie star,
A beautiful, glamorous, radiant, ravishing movie star!

NARRATOR (*Looks at her, then speaks. The music continues under the following*) And that was the way Ella passed her days. (ELLA *pantomimes going through the streets toward home*) Every night after work she would go home to her lonely furnished room. (ELLA *pantomimes climbing flights of stairs and entering her room*) She'd rinse out her chimney brush, (*She does*) and sit all night in front of the TV, (*She switches on the TV set, sits, and settles back. The "Syncopated Clock" theme is heard*) and she'd think to herself . . .

ELLA (*Singing*)

I'd be so grateful
That after premieres
I'd sweep out the theater
And fold up the chairs.
I would know what it meant
To be truly content
If I could only be a movie star.

(*The "Star Spangled Banner" starts.* ELLA *stands*

reverently for a moment, saluting, then turns off the set. The music continues; the lights fade on ELLA)

NARRATOR And that's how it was with Ella's life—working by day, dreaming by night. (*The lights go up on* ELLA *in her chimney*) Working. (*Work music;* ELLA *works briskly*) —and dreaming. (*The music stops;* ELLA *goes back to her room for dreaming*) Working—(*Music;* ELLA *goes back to the chimney for work*) —and dreaming. (ELLA *shoots an angry look at the* NARRATOR) Working. . . . Then one day Ella's employer came to her chimney with a sad expression on his face.

(*The* EMPLOYER, *a well-dressed man, enters; he goes to* ELLA*'s chimney and raps on it with his cane.* ELLA *rises to the top of the chimney, coughing*)

ELLA Don't do that. Oh, I'm sorry, Mr. Fallible.

EMPLOYER That's all right, Ella. It's good to know somebody's on the job, not goofing.

ELLA I don't see you in the chimney very often, sir.

EMPLOYER I don't get out in the field as often as I'd like. Ella, it's difficult for me to tell you this, but we won't need you after next week. Automation has come to chimney sweeping. I'm sorry.

NARRATOR Ella was unemployed.

EMPLOYER (*He leaves, taking the chimney with him*) You can keep the brushes.

NARRATOR For weeks Ella wandered the streets, looking for work. (ELLA *begins to wander the streets*) But nowhere was a good old-fashioned craftswoman needed. Winter came. (ELLA *bends into the wind and storm*) She began to go hungry. (ELLA *pantomimes hunger*) She began to fade away. (ELLA *sneezes*) Television was her only escape.

(ELLA *enters her room. During the following song, she shakes her piggy bank, switches on the TV set, and sings as through a severe headcold*)

ELLA (*Singing*)
Prospects look dismal,
How can I go on?
My piggy is empty,
My Kleenex is gone.
If I starve here alone,
Let them carve on my stone:
"She never got to be a movie star."

I'm not asking much. It's not as if I want to be a *rich* beautiful, glamorous movie star. Or even a *well-liked* beautiful, glamorous movie star. I just want to be a beautiful, glamorous movie star for its own sake. (*She sings*)
A beautiful, glamorous, radiant, ravishing
(*She sneezes*)
Mooo-vie star!

(ELLA *puts on her boots and exits*)

NARRATOR From the time she arrived home till the time she fell asleep, her eyes never wandered from the screen. Then one evening— (ELLA *returns to the room, hangs up her brush, and switches on the TV. She begins to sit in the armchair*) —it was the night of the full moon—

Ella returned from a thankless day of job-hunting, turned on the TV set—and there was no picture!

ELLA *(Pounding the set in panic)* No picture! No picture! No picture! No picture!

NARRATOR No picture. Stunned, disbelieving, she stood before the TV. Her eyes searched the screen for a trace of an image. *(She is crouching low, glaring into the set)* Then, Ella heard a voice. *(Electronic blips are heard as the TV glows weirdly)* Hello, out there! This is your friendly neighborhood Godmother! The program usually scheduled for this hour will not be seen. Instead, I have the pleasure to bring you the answer to your most cherished dream. Plink! *(The flashes go off)* Plank! *(The lights black out)* Plunk!

(More flashes. There is a blinding flash from the TV set. The music hits a dramatic climax. When the stage is visible again, ELLA *has been transformed into* PASSIONELLA. *She screams with delight and surprise as she sees the change in herself. The music to "Gorgeous" begins)*

PASSIONELLA *(Singing)*

Look at me! I am . . .
Gorgeous!
I am absolutely gorgeous.
Here's this avalanche of beauty
In one woman, and I'm it.
Look at the way all of the parts fit together!
Stunning!
See the way my nose stopped running!

I was positive this creature was there
Inside the old me,
All bottled up waiting to get free.

Now I see the real me;
Look at this! Look at that! Look at those!
Let me just feel me!
Beautiful, glamorous, radiant, ravishing,
Look at the hair!
Look at the shape!
Look everywhere!
(*She crosses to where the* NARRATOR *meets her*)
I am such a divine me!
(*He dances with her*)
Every studio will sign me.
My cup runneth over.
Who ever saw such a complete wow!
Nobody could say "No" to me now!
No one . . .
Is as . . .
Gorgeous
As I am!

NARRATOR (*Sitting down at his podium*) But be warned, my child. (*The weird music begins again;* PASSIONELLA *returns to her room*) Your friendly neighborhood Godmother has power only from Huntley-Brinkley to the Late Late Show. During those hours you shall be ravishing. You shall be Passionella. But only during those hours.

PASSIONELLA And the rest of the day?

NARRATOR The rest of the day, my dear, you shall be your usual, sooty self. This is your friendly neighborhood Godmother returning you to your local network.

(The music stops)

PASSIONELLA I have not a moment to lose!

NARRATOR Said Ella. And off she ran to El Morocco.

*(*PASSIONELLA *leaves the room. The room rolls off and a group of subway passengers enter. They are a motley group. The subway car stops and* PASSIONELLA *gets on; all heads turn to her. As the group sings the car crosses the stage)*

ALL *(Singing)*

Who, who, who, who, who
Is she?
Who is this ravishing sight?
With her fantasy face,
Her staggering smile,
Her indescribable bust?

Who is she?
She must be someone all right,
But who can she be?
Do you know?
Do you?

PASSENGER

No!

ALL

Then who, who, who, who
Is she?

And where's she off to tonight?
You'd think a chauffeur would drive
Her there in her
Private car!
Unless, of course, she's an
Underground movie star!
(*The car stops*)
Tell us who you are, ma'am.
Tell us who you are, ma'am.

PASSIONELLA (*Singing*)
I'm Passionella!

ALL
Passionella?

PASSIONELLA
Passionella, that's who I am!
(*The subway stops:* PASSIONELLA *gets off; the train goes on*)

ALL
That's who she am . . .
(PASSIONELLA *crosses to the El Morocco doorman who bows her into El Morocco. The chorus immediately re-enters as patrons of El Morocco*)

ALL
Who, who, who, who, who
Is she?
(*The orchestra continues the theme*)

PRODUCER I am a famous motion picture producer. Come

to my office tomorrow morning and I will sign you to a lifetime contract.

(*Photographers snap; flashbulbs pop;* PASSIONELLA *poses! The lights black out and a screen flies in*)

NARRATOR In the months that followed, a new star was born; the mysterious, exotic, bewitching temptress—Passionella. (*A movie is seen*) A legend grew around her. Strange stories circulated. Stories of how she would only allow her films to be shot between the hours of Huntley-Brinkley and the Late Late Show, and how at four A.M. she would hop into her sportscar and vanish. And, as the mystery grew, so did her popularity. Her pictures set new attendance records; she was in demand everywhere. And when there were no pictures to make, life became a ceaseless round of cocktail parties, premieres, and public appearances marked by frenzied adoration. Yes, Passionella had arrived!

(PASSIONELLA *bursts through a large photo of herself. She sings "I Know"*)

PASSIONELLA (*Singing*)

Look at me! I'm a
Movie star!
Every inch a movie star!
A beautiful, glamorous . . .

MAN I

Oh . . .

MAN I and 2

Oh . . .

MAN 1, 2, and 3

Oh . . .

MAN 1, 2, 3, and 4

Oh . . .

MAN 1, 2, 3, 4, and 5

Oh . . .
Passionella, how I love you!

PASSIONELLA

I know.

MEN (*Together*)

If you knew how I adore you!

PASSIONELLA

I know.

MAN 1

I can't sleep at night for thinking about you!

PASSIONELLA

It's understandable.

MAN 2

I want you.

MAN 3

I want you.

MEN

I want you.

PASSIONELLA
It must be awful.

MAN 2
Did you know I stole your slippers?

PASSIONELLA
I knew.

MEN
Pictures of you fill my bedroom.

PASSIONELLA
Mine, too.

MEN
I don't love Sophia.
I don't love Bardot.
I love Passionella.

PASSIONELLA
I know.

GIRLS (*There are five of them*)
Passionella, you're my idol.

PASSIONELLA
Of course.

GIRLS
How I long to look like you do.

PASSIONELLA

You should.

SOLO GIRL

I've read every word they've printed about you.

PASSIONELLA

You're not the only one.

GIRLS

In private
You are me, I am you.

PASSIONELLA

That's what I'm here for.

1ST BOY and GIRL (*In canon*)

As a goddess you're immortal.

2ND BOY and GIRL

Goddess, you're immortal.

3RD BOY and GIRL

You're immortal.

4TH BOY and GIRL

Mortal.

ALL

Oh . . .

PASSIONELLA

That's . . .

ALL *(In canon)*
Let me touch your sacred body.
Oh!

PASSIONELLA Well . . .

ALL
We'll be right there waiting,
Passionella.
Everywhere you go,
Passionella.
You cannot escape us;
Beautiful,
Incredible,
Extraordinary,
Passionella!!!

NARRATOR But—was Passionella happy? Now that she had wealth, fame, fans, success, glamor and excitement —was she truly content? Let us hear the answer in her own words.

PASSIONELLA Isn't this what I wanted? Isn't this what we all want? *(The chorus exits as* PASSIONELLA *sings)*
Wealth—
How delicious to be surrounded
By the comforts and luxuries
That I've never known before.
Fame—
I'm a figure of world importance,
I'm the center of every crowd,
Who could ask for more?

Fans, fans, fans, fans, fans,
When I see my adoring public
I remember the girl I was,
All alone and on the shelf.

Success—
I was nothing and now I'm something,
I am envied by everyone.
I envy me myself.

Glamor and excitement.
Lucky me, a movie star,
I was made for caviar,
And that's what I've got.

My life
Is exactly what I wished for,
So of course
I must be truly content.
But I'm not.

What does it all mean, if I cannot have love? Oh, how hollow is all this beauty without the right man to share it with.

NARRATOR And then one day, Passionella met the right man. She met him on Hollywood's famed Sunset Strip at the opening of a new psychedelic drugstore. (*A statue is brought on, covered with a large cloth*) This man, a celebrated recording star, who combined the outspoken fervor of Patrick Henry, the barbaric yawp of Walt Whitman, the cracker-barrel irreverence of Will Rogers, the flamboyant symbolism of Dylan Thomas, the swashbuckling elegance of Errol Flynn, the skeptical toughness of Bogart, the rugged earthiness of Brando, the sulky masculinity of Presley, the simple humanity of Roy Rogers, the zany vitality of the Beatles, the compassionate arrogance of Bob Dylan, and the hairstyle of Eleanor Roosevelt, had spoken to the hearts of discontented Americans everywhere. In short, he was the idol of millions: Flip, the Prince, Charming.

(The covering over the statue drops off, revealing FLIP. *A mob of admirers enters screaming wildly. They lift* FLIP *off the pedestal and carry him. The crowd quiets as he reaches the floor)*

NARRATOR For Passionella it was love at first sight.

FLIP *(Staring down at* PASSIONELLA*)* You dig Allen Ginsberg, man?

PASSIONELLA Who?

NARRATOR Beauty did not interest Flip.

FLIP You dig Timothy Leary?

PASSIONELLA Who? Who?

NARRATOR Glamor did not interest Flip.

FLIP You dig Harley-Davidson?

PASSIONELLA *(Looking around in confusion)* Who? Who? Who?

NARRATOR Only one thing interested Flip.

FLIP Reality, man. Truth. Soul. No woman is gonna

crack my soul without she is real. Somewhere, she waits, down there, close to the soil among the real people. Real!

CROWD Real!

NARRATOR Real!

PASSIONELLA But I *am* Real!

FLIP (*Leading her*) Dear lady, I am not getting through. Let me draw you a picture. (*He sings, holding a microphone he has in his pocket*)

The newspapers call you
The goddess of sex.
If you are a goddess,
I'm Oedipus Rex.
Neither goddess nor woman,
You're something apart,
With a cinerama body
And a celluloid heart.
Instead of a soul
You got a sign, sayin'
Decor by Helena Rubinstein.

(*He crosses behind her as the chorus closes in and surrounds her*)

ALL

How does it feel
To be the world's ideal,
When you know an' I know
That you are not real–real–real,
You are not real.

FLIP

The sons of old Adam
Have reason to grieve
Since we took a look at
You daughters of Eve.
You don't know what's honest,
You don't know what's true;
I'll tell you what's real,
It's the least I can do.
Dirty fingernails is real,
An' strag-ga-ly hair,
An' slovenly clothes,
An' a air of despair.

ALL (*Closing in on her as* FLIP *twirls his mike wire*)

How does it feel
To be the world's ideal,
When you know an' I know
That you are not real—real—real,
You are not real.

FLIP (*They have pushed her to the left of him. He is puffing a cigarette*)

I'm a-weary of glamor
An' women like you.
I long for a woman
Who's real through and through.
No goddess will ever
Get my heart to throb,
For the girl of my dreams
Is a slob.

ALL (*They form a single line across the stage and advance*

toward the audience. FLIP *forces* PASSIONELLA *through them)*

How does it feel
To be the world's ideal,
When you know an' I know
That you are not real.
How does it feel
To be the world's ideal,
When you know an' I know
That you are not—
You are not—
You are not—
Real!

(FLIP *throws his cigarette down and the crowd stamps it out as the lights black out)*

NARRATOR The next day Passionella went to the head of her studio.

(The lights restore to reveal the PRODUCER *sitting behind his desk)*

PASSIONELLA I am tired of being a cardboard figure on a tinsel background.

NARRATOR She said.

PRODUCER Oh!

NARRATOR Said the studio head.

PASSIONELLA I yearn to portray one of the real people.

NARRATOR She said.

PRODUCER Oh!

NARRATOR Said the studio head.

PASSIONELLA I want to play a chimney-sweep.

NARRATOR She said.

PRODUCER Oh!

NARRATOR Said the studio head. So there it was, and there was nothing anybody could do about it.

PASSIONELLA If I cannot play a chimney-sweep, I shall retire from the screen.

(She exits)

NARRATOR So the studio gave in. (*The* PRODUCER *holds his head in his hands and the lights black out*) "The Chimney-Sweep," a touching tale of simple people, was budgeted as a twenty-million-dollar production.

NEWSBOY (*Carrying some newspapers*) Extra! Extra! Glamor Girl to portray Chimney-Sweep! Passionella will sweep all her own chimneys!

NARRATOR Said the World-Journal-Herald-Globe-Eagle. Then came the most astonishing announcement of all— Passionella had insisted on a daytime shooting schedule! The entire free world, with the exception of France, reeled back, stunned. On the first day of shooting, the eyes of six continents fastened on a secluded set in the Hollywood Hills. (*The lights restore on a Hollywood set. There is a chimney and a movie dolly; many stagehands and extras are milling about)* Half a state had gathered to see the new Passionella arrive at the studio.

STAGEHAND Here comes the car.

(There is general hub-bub. An auto pulls up and ELLA *steps out covered by a huge cloak. She throws it off and the crowd gasps. She crosses to the chimney and begins sweeping)*

PRODUCER *(Weeping)* Marvelous! Not since Paul Muni!

NARRATOR Cried the producer.

DIRECTOR *(Weeping)* This is sheer folk art.

NARRATOR Cried the director.

REPORTER *(Weeping)* At last, movies have come of age!

NARRATOR Cried a reporter from the *Saturday Review.*

GIRLS *(Singing)*

Movie star, every inch a movie star.

MEN

Like a shining light of truth she stands.

ALL

This truly remarkable,
Sensitive, luminous.

(The chimney begins to roll offstage and they follow—the camera is brought in)

Movie star!

(They exit. The set flies out and a huge replica of an Oscar rolls on, carrying FLIP*)*

FLIP May I have the envelope, please, monkey? *(A starlet enters. She hands* FLIP *an Oscar and an envelope. They hug; she exits)* And the winner, for her performance in "The Chimney-Sweep"—Passionella!

(There is tumultuous cheering as PASSIONELLA *enters down the theater aisle and onto the stage)*

PASSIONELLA *(Hugging* FLIP *and the Oscar)* Ladies and gentlemen . . . *(The cheering fades. She is laughing and sobbing, hardly able to control herself)* Excuse me—this is the happiest—I'm sorry—I never imagined— Oh, I'm having a nervous breakdown . . . *(She falls on* FLIP *and finally recovers remarkably)* I would like to thank my producor *(sic)* and my director for their faith and encouragement. And most of all I would like to thank Mr. Charming, whose humanity and wisdom was my constant source of information. Oh, I'm so embarrassed. . . .

(She falls into FLIP'*s arms)*

FLIP And I want to take this opportunity to tell all you film fakers, that this little gal has shown you the way. Passionella, I love you, man. *(She gasps audibly)* Will you marry me?

PASSIONELLA *(Overcome)* Oh, Flip! The Oscar *and* you! Oh! Oh! *(She hugs him and turns into the microphone)*

I must be the luckiest girl in the world! (*To* FLIP) Yes, yes, yes! I'll marry you!

(*The lights black out*)

NARRATOR Dreamy-eyed, the two lovers went home, where, alone at last, they passed the night making tender love in front of the television set. (*The lights restore and we are in Bel-Air, the home of* PASSIONELLA. *There is a couch facing upstage, and a huge TV set which the audience can also view. There is a movie of Garbo's "Camille" in progress.* FLIP *and* PASSIONELLA *are in a tender embrace. The movie ends and the Late Late Show sign-off appears*) —and then. That completes our day's programming. This is your Late Late Show signing off. It was four A.M. (*They sit bolt upright*) Passionella was aghast! And then— (*She rises, facing upstage, obviously in great agitation.* FLIP *jumps up*) Plink! Plank! Plunk!

(*The lights black out and there is a huge flash. The lights restore and the stage is empty*)

ELLA (*Appearing behind the couch and dressed as she was in the beginning*) Flip? Flip? Flip?

(*She is shyly looking about.* FLIP *appears as a mousy, shy man from behind the other end of the couch. They see each other and cry out in surprise. They laugh and giggle.* FLIP *points to the TV set and pantomimes if that was she before watching with him. She agrees. The music begins*)

FLIP Were you . . . ?

(*He pantomimes the large bosom*)

ELLA (*Nods "Yes"*) Were you . . . ?
(*She pantomimes the huge head of hair*)

FLIP (*Nods "Yes"*) Imagine that.

ELLA I never would have guessed.

FLIP I know. I know. (*Singing*)
Here we are.

ELLA
The star

FLIP
And the star.

ELLA
Well, it just goes to show.

FLIP
We were some pair.
Me with my crazy hair

ELLA
Me with my solid gold gown.

FLIP
What's your name?

ELLA (*Speaking*) Ella. What's yours?

FLIP (*Singing*)
George L. Brown.

ELLA (*Speaking*) Oh, I love brown!

(*They slowly and shyly move to each other. They embrace*)

NARRATOR And they lived happily ever after.

(*The national anthem is heard, the screen showing the flag flying in bright colors. The* NARRATOR *rises and salutes*)

Curtain